What If You Met a Pirate?

An historical voyage of seafaring speculation
written & illustrated by
Jan Adkins

Roaring Brook Press
Brookfield, Connecticut

What if you met a pirate?

He'd be swinging a cutlass and clutching a dagger. He'd have pistols hanging all over him. He'd have a wooden leg and an eye patch. Of course he'd wear silver-buckled boots (well, one boot) and a fancy jacket with a feathered spangle hat. Surely he'd have a parrot on his shoulder, swearing and shrieking "Pieces of eight!"

And talk about ugly! If you met a pirate, he'd have scars and nasty, bushy eyebrows over wicked little pig eyes (well, one eye). Disgusting! But he'd certainly wear a gold ring in his ear and jeweled rings on every finger, and he'd have a scented hanky sticking out of his lace sleeve.

Hoo boy! If you met a pirate, you'd be in a tight spot! What could you do?

Well, the best advice might be to run.

Run?

Sure. That pirate can't be very fast with a wooden leg. He can't see very well with one eye. If he's holding a cutlass and a dagger, he can't get those big pistols out without dropping everything. Even if he did grab the pistols, the parrot and all those rings would get in the way. He'd probably shoot his other foot.

Pirates like this couldn't really be very successful. But he looks like a pirate, doesn't he? You know what pirates look like because you've seen them in movies and books, right?

Three-cornered hat with egret
feather, very expensive

Silken kerchief
Gold earring
Big beard and long, wavy hair, like a
shampoo commercial

Flashing smile
Fancy lace-trimmed shirt
Embroidered waistcoat
Colorful, rich coat

Many pistols

Dagger

Parrot

Long sword

Jeweled rings

Silken sash

Fancy breeches
Extra dagger
High leather boot with silver buckle

Wooden peg leg

What If You Met a Pirate?   3

How would you know a real pirate?

Real pirates weren't flashy dressers. They looked like common sailors because, actually, they were.

They were seagoing bandits, smugglers, and for many countries in times of war (certainly for England and the United States), they were a ragtag private navy. But how much time did a pirate spend on pirating? Not much.

Most of the time, pirates were plain simple sailors. A fortunate pirate might swashbuckle just a few hours each month. The rest of his time was taken up with the work of sailing a ship, pumping water out of the ship, repairing the ship, patching the ship's sails, painting things on the ship, and pulling the ship's ropes. Ships had to be sailed from one pirating job to the next, through brutal tropical heat and wicked cold. Sailors climbed into the rigging to manage the sails at noon, at night, in rain squalls and even hurricanes.

The work was hard, monotonous, dirty, and dangerous. Some pirates died from drowning or in accidents. Most died from disease, especially in the tropics. Pirates who died in battles were rare, but not as rare as old pirates.

If you met a real pirate, the first thing that would impress you would probably be how shabby and dirty he was. The second thing would almost certainly be his smell. Pirates didn't take baths. Fresh water was precious aboard a ship, and saltwater doesn't clean people or clothes well. Stinky fellows.

A CROWDED SHIP *is a tight little village. Pirates helped one another with every kind of work. Men proud of their long pigtails chose "tie mates" to do their braiding.*

PLENTY OF PIRATES *had an arm or leg taken off by gunfire or an accident. If they lived, they usually gave up the pirate's life; sailing and climbing into the rigging are hard. Some one-legged sailors, however, were allowed to become cooks.*

Felt hats were too expensive; most pirates wore a cloth cap or a bandanna tied around the head.

Sailing is a dangerous business, even without firing cannon. Wind whipped ropes around, storms threw sailors around. Many pirates lost an eye and covered the wound with an eye patch. Pirates often had terrible scars for the same reason.

Most pirates had bad teeth, and not very many of them.

A wool jacket was comfortable on chilly days or nights. Sometimes pirates (and other sailors) sewed their own jackets of heavy cotton canvas and colored them with a blue vegetable dye called indigo.

A plain cotton or linen shirt, neatly patched and old. Sailors were very good at sewing repairs in sails or clothes.

Wool or cotton canvas trousers, loose and easy to roll up, also patched. Also very dirty. It's hard to wash clothes in saltwater, and fresh water on an ocean-going ship is always precious.

Pirates smelled. A lot. They never took baths (which weren't considered healthy), they sweated a lot, and they probably owned only two or three pieces of (unwashed) clothing.

For safer footing up in the rigging, pirates worked barefoot. Belowdecks, they might wear felt slippers.

Gold earrings had a purpose: If a sailor fell overboard and drowned (most couldn't swim), then washed ashore, the gold ring paid the cost of burying his body with a church service and a headstone.

Sailors had trouble with lice or fleas in their hair; sometimes they cut it very short. An experienced sailor, however, might take pride in his long, braided pigtail, sometimes covered by a tanned eelskin.

A pirate's bandanna was not a lacey decoration. He used it to blow his nose, wipe off sweat, and wipe his greasy hands and everything else.

Pirates might wear a ring ashore but not at sea. Rings might catch in the rigging and pull off a finger. Even without rings, many pirates lost fingers.

Pirates didn't carry swords, daggers, or pistols unless they were attacking a ship. Most sailors carried a short knife to cut line and canvas; they also ate with it. Some captains broke off the points of sailors' knives so they couldn't fight among themselves with them.

Pirates sometimes owned parrots bought in Africa or South America. Unusual birds could be resold for a good price in a port town. On board a ship, cats were more useful—they caught rats.

What If You Met a Pirate? 5

Who got to be a pirate?

Pirates were sea robbers. They stole from other ships or used a pirate ship to steal from seaside towns. But you'd never walk onto the dock and ask for a pirate! They were very touchy about that name. Most pirates had letters of marque (say mark). Letters of marque were fancy documents from Country A, authorizing a pirate ship to steal from Country B—if they gave half of the booty to Country A. With these papers, a pirate ship became a "private warship," or privateer. Pirates were hanged, but privateers were official. From their share of the booty—anything they stole—privateers paid for their own ships, sails, paint, guns, and supplies, and they paid their own men. Giving pirates letters of marque was a cheap way for a country to build up its navy.

Being a pirate was a strange way to make a living, but it was better than being in England's Royal Navy. Navy sailors worked very hard, weren't allowed to talk on deck, ate awful food, and were often not paid or allowed to go ashore for years. Because England needed a large navy, it was legal to "press" new sailors—to kidnap men walking down the street or sitting in a tavern. These press-men might never see their homes or families again. If sailors disobeyed in the smallest way, they were usually flogged—tied up and beaten. Many sailors who ran away from the Royal Navy became pirates.

Being a pirate was, in some ways, better than most jobs. Between 1500 and 1750, a pirate or privateer ship was the only real democracy: The entire crew voted on important questions. A pirate captain was elected by his own men, and they could fire him.

On shore, pirates might be wild, but at sea there were strict rules. Each crew member made his mark—sometimes in blood—on a written contract. By signing, he promised to obey the rules: no gambling, drunkenness, fighting, stealing (from one another), or sleeping on duty. Everyone shared equally, although those with special skills—like a gunner or carpenter—got a little extra. And no women were allowed on board. Piracy was pretty much a guy thing. Of the thousands of pirates we know about, only a few were women.

FLOGGING *was the Royal Navy punishment for anything from talking out loud on deck to taking too much time to climb the mast. The offending sailor was tied up and whipped with the cat o' nine tails. This type of whip had nine hard cords, and each cord had three hard knots. Ouch! Each ship kept its cat in a special red cloth bag. This is where we get our phrase "the cat is out of the bag," meaning that something grim is about to happen.*

PRIVATEERS & PIRATES, *what's the difference? Not much. Only a piece of paper, the letter of marque. Pirates were working for themselves, but privateers shared half their booty with the government that wrote its letter of marque.*

PIRATE

PRIVATEER

CRUELTY & DRUDGERY

in the Royal Navy made many sailors run away—sometimes to a life of piracy. After being flogged and forced to follow harsh rules and cruel officers, life aboard a pirate ship looked easy, and more profitable. When a sailor deserted the Royal Navy, his name was marked on navy lists with an R for "run." He could never return without being severely punished. Perhaps this is why most pirates took another, more fanciful name, like Calico Jack or Billy Bowlegs.

Where could you find a pirate if you needed one?

Chinese pirate

PACIFIC OC

CHINESE PIRATES in the South China seas have been troublesome for eight centuries. A beautiful pirate queen, Lai Chou San, commanded a fleet of heavily armed junks until 1937, when modern Japanese destroyers wiped them out. Container ships and private yachts are still attacked in the narrow Malacca Straits.

Mecca

Bombay

Canton

Manila

SOUTH CHINA SEA

Malacca Strait

BARRATARIA, an enormous swamp kingdom in the Mississippi Delta, was ruled by the pirate Jean Lafitte from 1805 to 1821. He smuggled luxuries tax-free into fashionable New Orleans, defying customs officials and the tiny United States Navy. But this curiously patriotic American pirate plundered only Spanish ships. During the War of 1812, Lafitte and his force of men helped Andrew Jackson defeat British invaders at the Battle of New Orleans.

Pirate Round

THE PIRATE ROUND was the trip from the Atlantic Ocean, around the Cape of Good Hope, up to bases in Madagascar. On the Indian Ocean, the Red Sea, and the Arabian Sea in the 17th and 18th centuries, pirates called freebooters snapped up dhows filled with wealthy Muslim pilgrims bound to and from Mecca and captured Indian vessels carrying gold, silk, and spices.

MADAGASCAR

INDIAN OCEAN

MADAGASCAR was a pirate haven from the 16th to the 18th century. Pirates from Christian nations in the West believed that raiding Muslim and Hindu vessels was not a real crime—and it was very profitable.

Cape of Good Hope

THE SPANISH MAIN was the Central and South American mainland. In the 16th and 17th centuries, at treasure ports such as Maracaibo, Cartagena, Portobelo, and Colón, gold seized from the native Aztecs and Incas was loaded onto galleons bound for Spain.

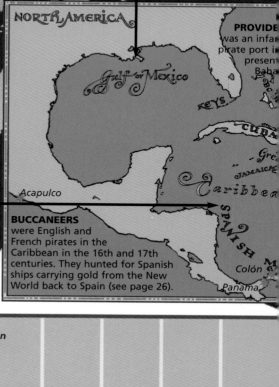

NORTH AMERICA

Gulf of Mexico

KEYS

CUBA

Bahá

PROVIDE
was an infam
pirate port i
present

Gre
JAMAICA

Caribbea

Acapulco

SPANISH

Colón

Panama

BUCCANEERS were English and French pirates in the Caribbean in the 16th and 17th centuries. They hunted for Spanish ships carrying gold from the New World back to Spain (see page 26).

A pirate timeline

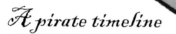

78 BC
Julius Caesar captured by Mediterranean pirates

Fleets of Mediterranean pirates raid grain and wine vessels

1	100	200	300	400	500	600	700	800	900	10

Viking pirates active

Finding a pirate depends on when as much as where. When there were wars, there were plenty of pirates and privateers. When peace returned, pirates went back to other jobs. Even today, there are still pirates skulking in the backwaters of the seas.

Viking pirate

VIKINGS, skillful sailors from Norway, Denmark, and Sweden, raided shore towns in the 8th to 12th centuries. Englishmen had a special prayer: "And from the fury of the Norsemen, Lord deliver us!"

London

FRENCH CORSAIRS were privateers who snapped up merchant vessels of England and Spain in the 17th and 18th centuries.

Cádiz

MEDITERRANEAN

Barbary Coast

THE SEADOGS were English privateers sent out to raid the Spanish by Queen Elizabeth I in the 16th century (see page 24).

American Colonies

Boston
New York

ANCIENT PIRATES swarmed all over the Mediterranean. In 78 BC, Julius Caesar was captured and held for ransom by pirates. The ransom was paid, he went free—but he returned to execute all the pirates in the band.

BARBARY CORSAIRS were Muslim pirates from the Barbary Coast of North Africa. They preyed on Christian ships and towns between the 11th and 19th centuries.

THE BLACK SHIP was a famous prize of the 16th and 17th centuries. It was the Manila Galleon, a treasure ship that sailed once a year. To avoid pirates, the galleon was forbidden to stop until it reached the fortress of Acapulco. The long voyage was a trial. Crews were reduced by starvation and scurvy, sometimes leaving only a few dozen men to work the ship.

CARIBBEAN

Hispaniola

Acapulco

NORTH ATLANTIC OCEAN

GULF of GUINEA

FREEBOOTERS (see page 28) were American, English, and French pirates who sailed the Pirate Round, attacking Spanish treasure galleons in the Caribbean and smuggling goods and slaves into the American colonies.

HISPANIOLA, now Haiti and the Dominican Republic, was a pirate haven during the 17th and 18th centuries. It was home to the infamous Brotherhood of the Coast, a loose pirate navy raiding Spanish treasure galleons and the ports of the Spanish Main.

HISPANIOLA

Lesser Antilles

Sea

Maracaibo

gena

SOUTH AMERICA

SOUTH ATLANTIC OCEAN

Pirate Round

Cape Horn

DURING THE CRUSADES—the "Holy Wars" between Christians and Muslims from the 10th to the 14th centuries—there were always plenty of pirates on both sides.

Barbary corsair

Captain Nathaniel Gordon, last American pirate, hanged

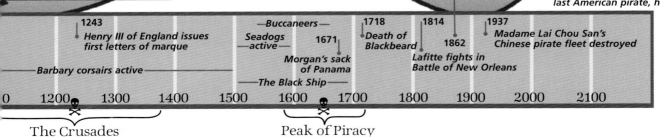

	1243		Buccaneers	1718	1814	1937	
	Henry III of England issues first letters of marque	Seadogs active	1671	Death of Blackbeard	1862	Madame Lai Chou San's Chinese pirate fleet destroyed	
Barbary corsairs active			Morgan's sack of Panama		Lafitte fights in Battle of New Orleans		
			The Black Ship				
0	1200	1300	1400	1500	1600	1700	1800	1900	2000	2100

The Crusades   Peak of Piracy

What did a pirate ship look like?

You've seen pirate movies. The pirate captain and his crew of jolly, singing sailors travel around in a big ship with a lot of big guns, looking for Spanish galleons stuffed with treasure and commanded by evil Spanish lords with pointy beards and big, flouncy hats. When the captain sights a likely looking galleon, he sails up beside it and demands that the evil captain surrender. Naturally, Don Nastioso refuses. Then comes the battle, very loud. The two ships fight, broadside to broadside. Things explode. The evil Spanish lord dies with a sneer on his lips.

Forget about the movies.

Pirates didn't want big ships, and they didn't want to fight at all. They were smarter than that. They hid in shallow rivers and marshes, so they needed small boats that weren't very deep. They darted out—very often at night—and took larger boats by surprise, so they needed fast, easy to maneuver ships. Pirates wanted weather boats—usually sloops or schooners that could sail closer to the direction of the wind than the heavy, square-rigged warships sent to capture them (see page 12).

Pirates didn't make long voyages like the Royal Navy. Their trips were short, often only a few days. Pirates didn't want to match their little boats' guns with the navy's big guns, so they counted on surprise, a lot of men, and boarding the prize in a yelling, furious rush. When they traveled, pirates were packed into small boats like dogs in a kennel.

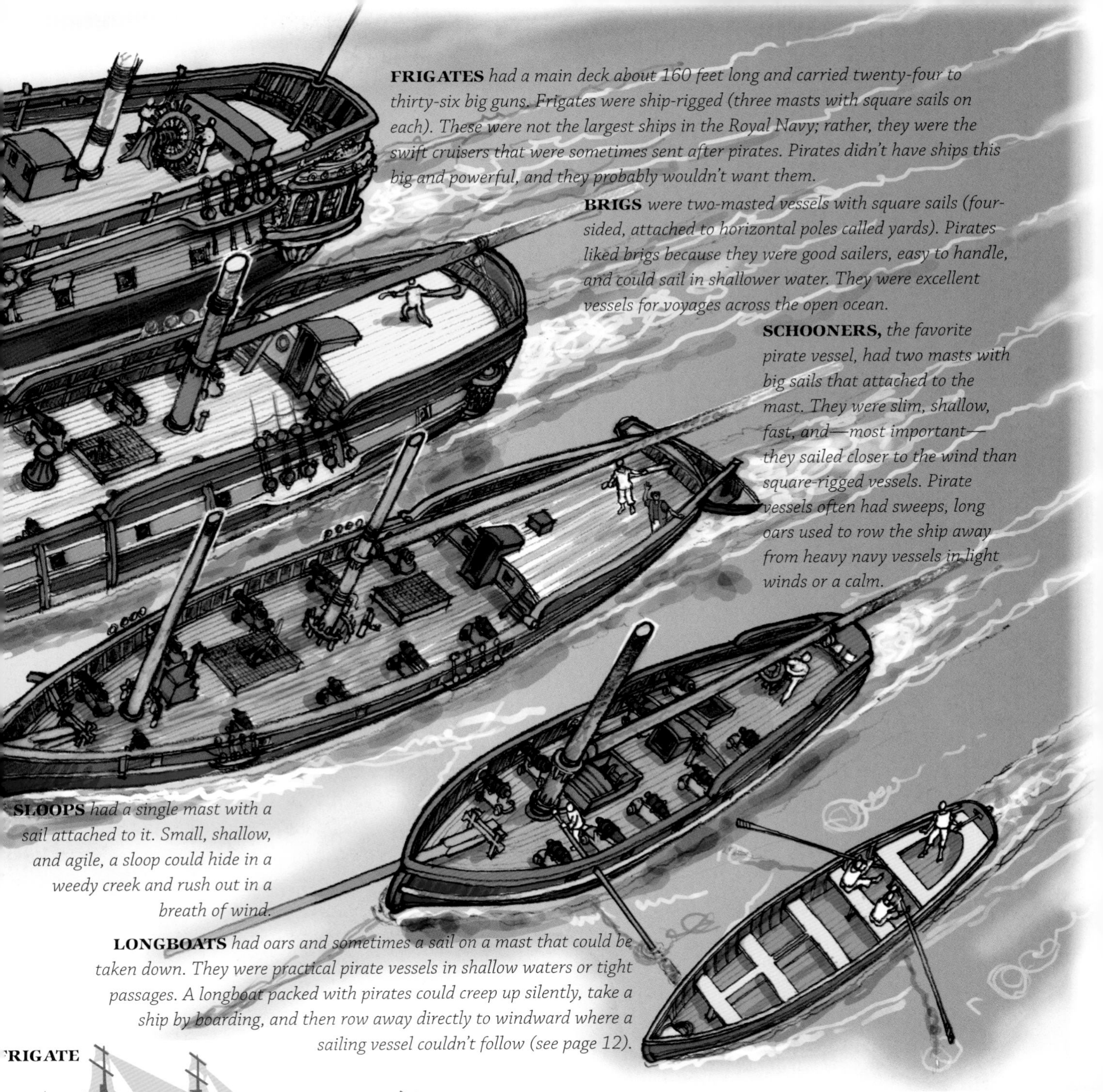

FRIGATES *had a main deck about 160 feet long and carried twenty-four to thirty-six big guns. Frigates were ship-rigged (three masts with square sails on each). These were not the largest ships in the Royal Navy; rather, they were the swift cruisers that were sometimes sent after pirates. Pirates didn't have ships this big and powerful, and they probably wouldn't want them.*

BRIGS *were two-masted vessels with square sails (four-sided, attached to horizontal poles called yards). Pirates liked brigs because they were good sailers, easy to handle, and could sail in shallower water. They were excellent vessels for voyages across the open ocean.*

SCHOONERS, *the favorite pirate vessel, had two masts with big sails that attached to the mast. They were slim, shallow, fast, and—most important— they sailed closer to the wind than square-rigged vessels. Pirate vessels often had sweeps, long oars used to row the ship away from heavy navy vessels in light winds or a calm.*

SLOOPS *had a single mast with a sail attached to it. Small, shallow, and agile, a sloop could hide in a weedy creek and rush out in a breath of wind.*

LONGBOATS *had oars and sometimes a sail on a mast that could be taken down. They were practical pirate vessels in shallow waters or tight passages. A longboat packed with pirates could creep up silently, take a ship by boarding, and then row away directly to windward where a sailing vessel couldn't follow (see page 12).*

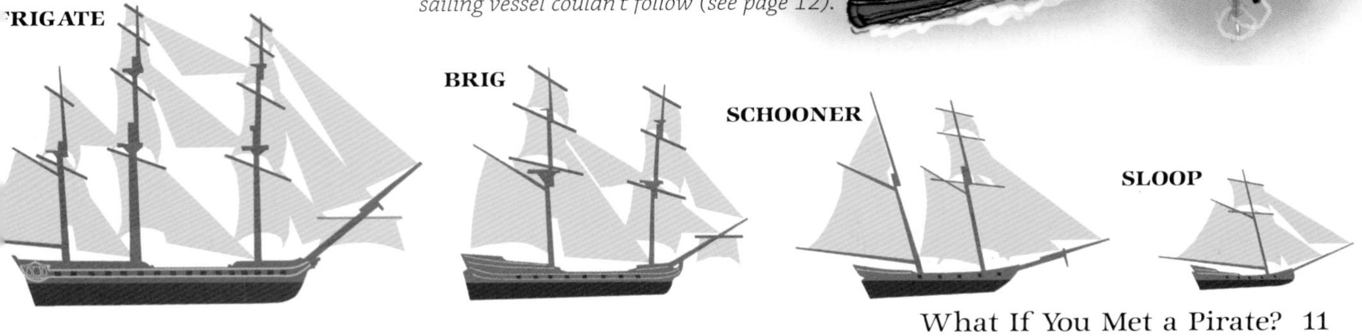

FRIGATE

BRIG

SCHOONER

SLOOP

How did pirate ships sail?

Pirates were scalawags and scoundrels but, mostly, they were sailors. They were clever planners, too. They chose fast, nimble ships that could swoop quickly down on merchant vessels and get away from men o' war trying to catch them.

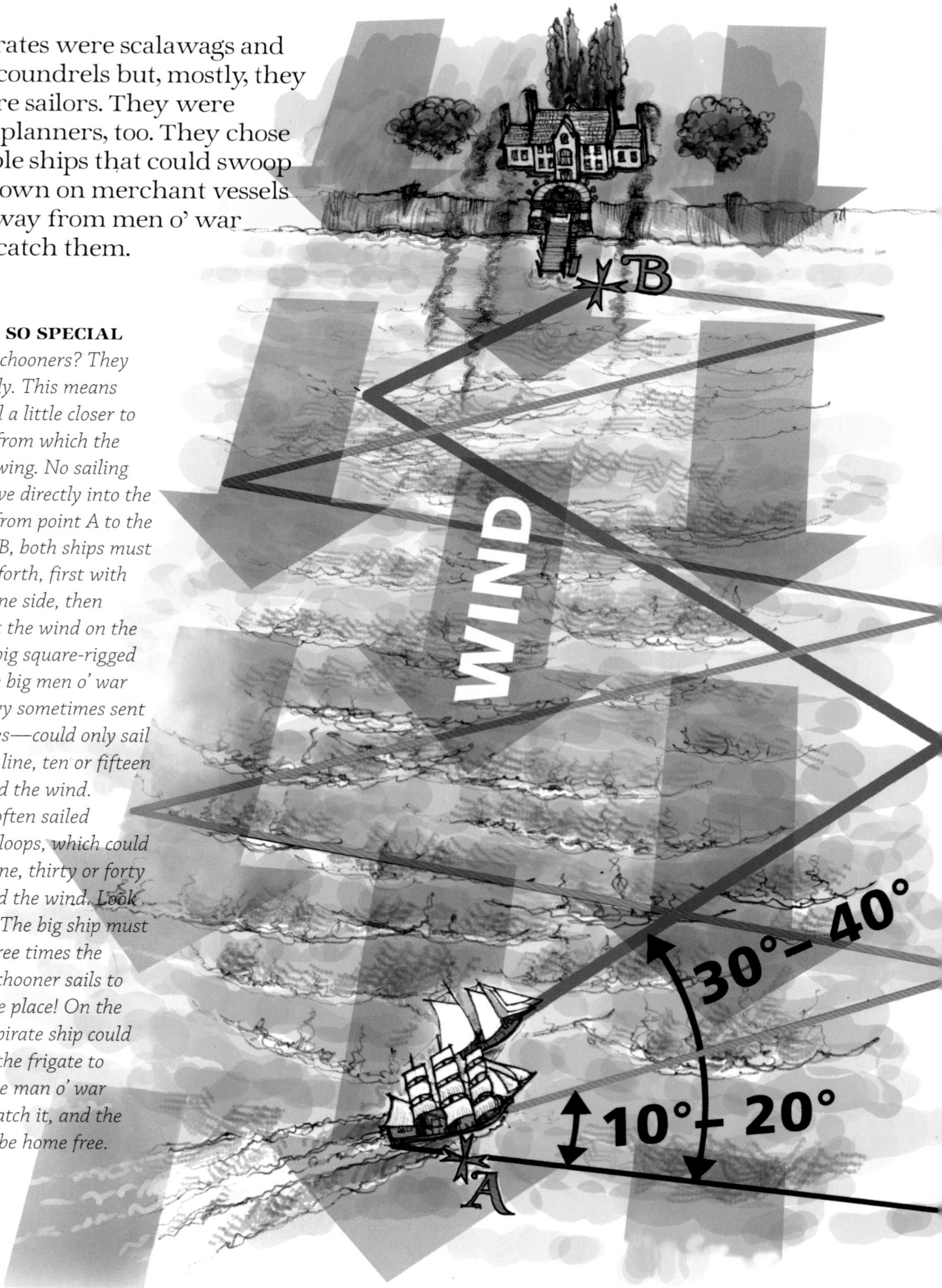

WHAT WAS SO SPECIAL *about pirate schooners? They were weatherly. This means they could sail a little closer to the direction from which the wind was blowing. No sailing vessel can move directly into the wind. To get from point A to the dock at point B, both ships must sail back and forth, first with the wind on one side, then turning to put the wind on the other side. A big square-rigged ship—like the big men o' war the Royal Navy sometimes sent to catch pirates—could only sail on the orange line, ten or fifteen degrees toward the wind. Pirates more often sailed schooners or sloops, which could sail the blue line, thirty or forty degrees toward the wind. Look at the angles! The big ship must sail almost three times the distance the schooner sails to reach the same place! On the open sea, the pirate ship could easily outrun the frigate to windward. The man o' war would never catch it, and the pirates would be home free.*

B

WIND

30° – 40°

10° – 20°

A

STEERING WHEELS *were rope winches that turned the big steering rudder at the stern (the back) of the ship. The rudder turned the boat to the right (starboard) or the left (port). Larger ships had two or three steering wheels attached to this winch. When a storm was hammering at the rudder, four or six men might struggle to steer. Knowing where they were on the trackless ocean meant life or death for sailors, so there was no fooling around for the men on duty at the wheel. They watched the compass intently, steering a straight course, so the vessel's position could be plotted exactly. This work required so much concentration that the men at the wheel were normally changed every hour.*

SMALLER IS BETTER. *Draft—how deep in the water a vessel floats—was especially important for pirates. Big warships sent to capture pirates were usually deep-draft vessels that couldn't chase the smaller pirate schooners and sloops into "thin water"—the small harbors and shallow creeks where pirates hid. Shallow-draft pirates might also escape across shallow reefs that would tear the man o' war's bottom out.*

DID PIRATES GET SEASICK? *Almost everyone gets seasick now and then, mostly at the beginning of a voyage. The awful feeling usually goes away in time. When sailors were seasick during a storm, there was nothing to do but throw up and keep sailing. After a long voyage, sailors had become so accustomed to the motion of a ship that walking on the solid land could make them landsick!*

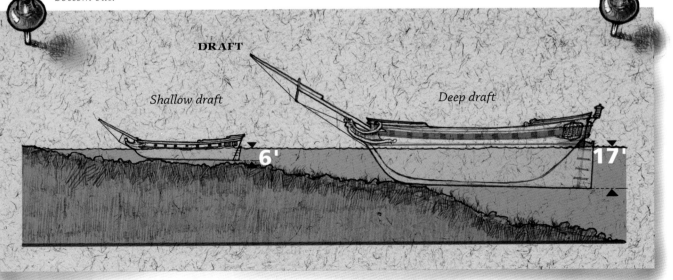

DRAFT

Shallow draft   *Deep draft*

6'   17'

What did pirates do all day?

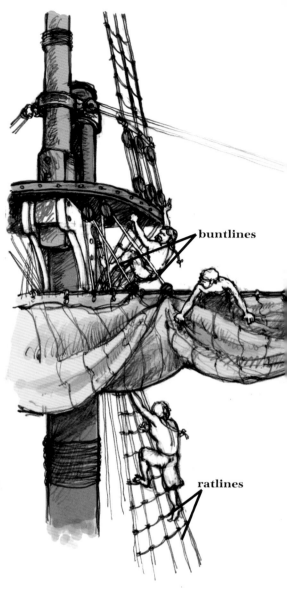

buntlines

ratlines

THEY WORKED. HARD. When the weather changed, they changed the sails. If the wind died down, the sailors would put out more sail. If the wind got stronger, sailors would take in some sail. If the weather changed directions, sailors would take in these sails and put out those to balance the vessel. This went on all day and all night. Pulling up heavy canvas sails was real work. Buntlines were used to haul up parts of the sail like a curtain. This took the wind pressure out of the sail. Then sailors climbed ratlines (the rope "ladders" at the sides) and shuffled out on foot ropes to pull up the rest of the sails and furl them—tie them to the yards. They could also take up only part of the sail, making a smaller sail for high winds; this was called reefing the sail.

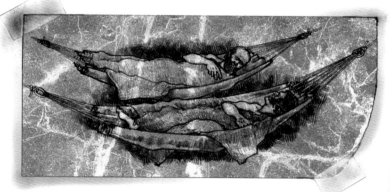

YOU CAN'T STOP at night on the ocean. Offshore, part of the crew sailed the ship while part of the crew slept. Sailors slept in hanging cloth beds, hammocks, which rocked to and fro as the ship rolled.

SHIPS LEAK, every one of them, especially old wooden ones. A part of every pirate's day was spent pumping water out of the bilge, the deepest part of the hull.

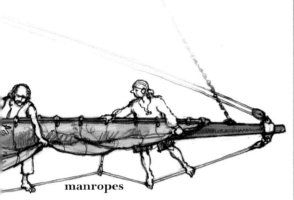

manropes

FOOD *on a pirate vessel was kept in barrels. Pirates had no refrigerators. Their meat was beef or pork preserved in very salty water. They fished from the boat's rail. They hunted sea turtles on the beach. Their bread was a dried brown biscuit called hardtack that kept for years. They ate cheese, oatmeal porridge sweetened with molasses and raisins, and dried peas boiled into a sticky mash. A favorite dessert was plum duff, made from crumbled biscuits, raisins, sugar, and spices. They drank beer and wine and grog (water mixed with rum). Salamagundi was the pirate's favorite dish, made from several kinds of meat, fish, and fowl cooked in spiced wine The cooked meat was simmered with cabbage, olives, pickled vegetables, hard-boiled eggs, onions, and mangos. It was seasoned with salt, garlic, red and black pepper, mustard seed, and vinegar. Hard to imagine, but it was considered a treat.*

molasses
oatmeal
salamagundi
dried peas
salt beef

hardtack   cheese   grog   beer   plum duff   peppers

GOING TO THE BATHROOM
wasn't difficult for pirates in calm weather. They went to the head—the front of the ship—where they sat, perched over the water, on a bench with holes (called the seat of ease). In rough weather, they used buckets.

What If You Met a Pirate?   15

irate life was hard but fair. Among pirates, unlike society ashore, each pirate had an equal share in decisions and in the booty. There were no noblemen, lords, or dukes aboard a pirate ship, and no one was called sir. But men with special skills did have special names.

BOSUN *is the short version of boatswain, which means the ship's husband. The bosun was an important man. He and his bosun's mates made sure everything from the tiniest pulley to the paint on the hull was in good order.*

THE MASTER *wasn't the captain. His special duty was navigation—knowing the vessel's location at all times. The master kept careful measurements of the vessel's course and speed. He used ocean charts and calculated the vessel's position at sea using the height of the sun and stars from the horizon, measured by devices like this quarterstaff. Close to shore he needed to know how deep the water was.*

THE LEADSMAN *stood in the forechains—the rigging at the base of the foremast. He threw a long line with a lead weight at the end, feeling the lead strike at the bottom. Then, reading the depth from marks on the line, he called it out to the Master.*

JACK O' THE DUST AND JEMMY DUCKS *were important at mealtimes. Jack kept the ship's biscuit safe, dry, and away from rats. Jemmy took care of the chickens and ducks often kept in a pen on deck.*

SAILS *made and repaired sails. Most sailors were handy with needle and thread, and they usually made their own clothes.*

COOPER *was the barrel maker. Everything pirates ate and drank was kept in these watertight containers.*

SPARKS *was the vessel's blacksmith, who made bolts and rings for the rigging and also took care of the cutlasses, pikes, and axes.*

CHIPS *was the vessel's carpenter. He repaired storm and battle damage, plugged holes, and kept the ship's small boats in good shape.*

GUNS *was the gunner, the expert in charge of the vessel's cannon, pistols, and muskets. He and his gunner's mates were the only men allowed in the magazine, the closed room where the gunpowder was kept. This room was lit through an inside window by a lamp outside the magazine—no flames near the powder! The gunner filled bags with the right amount of powder for each cannon.*

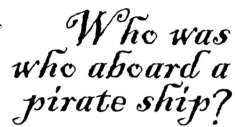

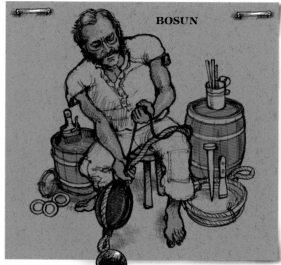

BOSUN

CHIPS

JACK O' THE DUST & JEMMY DUC

LEADSMAN

lead

"the chains"

quarterstaff

MASTER

GUNS

SPARKS

COOPER

SAILS

There was plenty of dangerous stuff aboard a pirate ship. Pirates liked short swords called cutlasses and scary boarding axes; both were easy to handle on crowded decks. Pikes were long staffs with points and, sometimes, hooks on the end. Pistols were okay for shooting, but there was no time to reload; still they were heavy, good for smashing heads. Muskets were used by sharpshooters placed high in the rigging; they aimed at the prize ship's captain and at the men who were steering the prize. Sometimes they used broad-mouthed shotguns called blunderbusses.

Pirate vessels didn't want to trade broadsides with a well-armed ship. Pirate cannon were aimed to cripple the prize without hurting it too much—pirates ransomed or sold back prizes for a lot of money. Cannon fired several kinds of shot, some meant to put holes in the prize's hull, some meant to cut up the prize's rigging so she couldn't sail away.

Some murderous shot—grape and canister—was meant to "sweep the decks" of fighting sailors on the prize. Bloody work. Pirates weren't as bloodthirsty as their legends would have you believe—but let's be truthful: They were violent, wicked criminals.

GRAPNELS *looked like four-pronged anchors. They were thrown to catch at a prize's rigging and haul it alongside so the pirates could get aboard.*

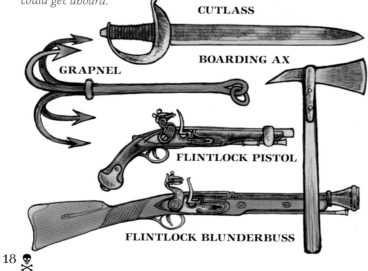

CUTLASS

GRAPNEL

BOARDING AX

FLINTLOCK PISTOL

FLINTLOCK BLUNDERBUSS

Enough cooking and sewing! What about cannon?

ROUND SHOT *got rusty. Before a raid, the rust had to be chipped away with hammers and the shot passed through a circle shot gauge to make sure it was still spherical and wouldn't wobble off aim when it was fired. Round shot was meant to put holes in the hull, knock away the rudder, destroy the steering wheel, or blow away the prize's cannon.*

BAR SHOT AND CHAIN SHOT *began to whirl as soon as they left the cannon's muzzle, screaming as they traveled toward the prize. Like spinning blades, they cut up the prize's rigging and disabled the vessel.*

GRAPE SHOT *was a package of several small balls—about the size of Ping-Pong balls—tied into a cloth bag. The bag burst as the cannon was fired and the balls spread. Grape shot cut up rigging and cut down sailors.*

CANISTER *was a can or cloth package holding hundreds of musket balls. It was used only at short range. There was only one reason for canister: The balls spread into a broad pattern of murder.*

CANNON *were dangerous to everyone, even the pirates who fired them. Even small cannon were extremely heavy. They were pulled up into the gunport with pulleys on both sides. The elevation (the up-and-down angle) was adjusted with wedge-shaped quoins. Cannon were aimed left or right by turning them with long levers called crows (our crowbars are the same kind of lever). To prime the cannon—to get it ready to fire—a priming wire was thrust down the vent to put a hole in the bag of powder; then the vent was filled with fine powder from a powder horn. The gun crew (four or five men) stepped back, and the gunner waited for the vessel to roll up on the waves. At the height of the roll, he dabbed the slow match (a long-burning cord) smoldering on the linstock against the powder in the touch hole. Boom! When it was fired, the cannon would recoil—shoot back fast with terrible force. Anyone in the way could be killed. The recoil was stopped by the heavy rope breeching.*

RELOADING *was tricky. The hot barrel had to be wiped out with a wet swab to get rid of any glowing bits of powder or fabric that could ignite the new powder while it was being thrust down the barrel with a rammer. Cloth wads were pushed into the barrel to make a tight seal; then the shot was rammed tight. The cannon was pulled back up into place and primed for the next shot. Occasionally a cannon simply blew up, killing the whole crew.*

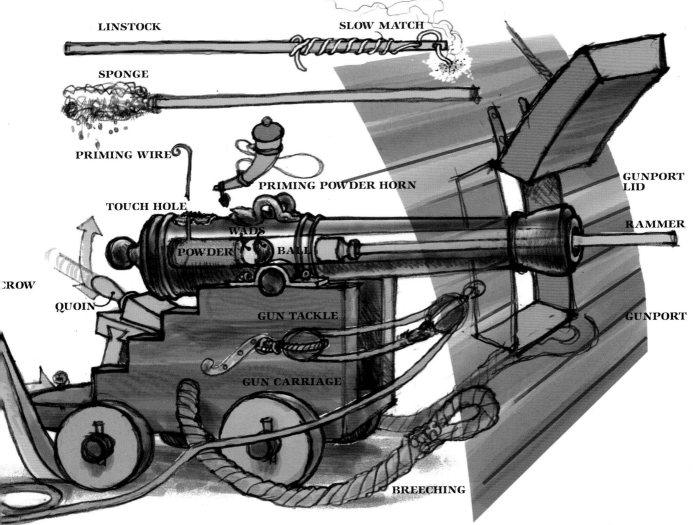

LINSTOCK

SLOW MATCH

SPONGE

PRIMING WIRE

PRIMING POWDER HORN

GUNPORT LID

TOUCH HOLE

RAMMER

WADS

POWDER BALL

CROW

QUOIN

GUN TACKLE

GUNPORT

GUN CARRIAGE

BREECHING

The real trick was to take a prize without getting a lot of people killed—your own pirates or the sailors on the prize. There were a couple of ways to do this. Surprise was the best: Sneak up on the prize as it sailed through a narrow passage at night, then swarm over the side of the ship, yelling like demons!

False flags disguised a pirate vessel. Pirates might fly the flag of a peaceful nation. They would hide men below as they sailed sweetly up to the prize. Sometimes pirates even dressed up like women and children to fool other ships!

When surprise wouldn't work, terrifying the prize's sailors might. Pirates spread tall tales about how angry and vicious they got when prizes didn't stop and surrender instantly. Vaporing was scary: The pirate crew danced around, banging their cutlasses together and shouting terrible threats, making rude gestures and singing awful songs. Wouldn't you be scared?

VAPORING

PIRATE FLAGS *were usually "false flags" of a peaceful nation, flown to fool unwary ships. If the pirates lost the advantage of surprise and actually chased a vessel, they might hoist two flags. The first was the red flag, called the* jolie rouge *in French (our "jolly roger" comes from this). This flag offered quarter: The officers and sailors could go free if they promised to pay a quarter of their next year's pay. (Folks took promises more seriously back then.)*

If the prize didn't stop, the pirates might hoist the no-more-Mr.-Nice-Guy black flag, sometimes but not always with a skull and crossed bones. This meant that if the prize didn't stop immediately, the pirates would kill everyone aboard. Would they? Maybe.

SPANISH FLAG

JOLIE ROUGE

BLACKBEARD'S FLAG

STINKPOTS were a special pirate weapon: clay jars, filled with sulfur and burning stuff, thrown into the ship's hold. What an awful smell! It drove sailors who were barricaded below onto the deck.

MERCY was profitable. Pirates didn't often kill prisoners. New sailors got the chance to join the pirate crew. If they chose not to join, pirates would put them ashore. People of any importance were ransomed: A message was sent demanding a lot of money for their freedom. Some pirates, certainly, were murderous thugs. Most of the famous pirates, however, were amazingly polite to captured women.

WALKING THE PLANK never happened. There is not a single record of it in the pirate accounts. This fanciful punishment was probably invented by a famous illustrator (like me) named Howard Pyle, who wrote and illustrated a book about pirates.

SURPRISE NIGHT ATTACK

GOLD & JEWELS **SUGAR** **SPICES**

*P*lunder, the stuff pirates stole, was not all silver and gold. Pirates took—or smuggled—anything they could find and anything that would sell. A pirate bazaar was a local celebration. A schooner or brig would sail into the town landing and set up shop on the dock. The prices were good because no taxes were being paid. These bazaars offered the locals a chance to buy foreign luxuries that English colonies weren't allowed to import. Jean Lafitte's pirate bazaars on the outskirts of New Orleans were social gatherings where you might see maids shopping for a pretty lace shawl and the governor's wife looking for rolls of Chinese silk.

What about plunder?

BLACKBIRDS *were illegally imported slaves. Outlaw pirates were more willing than most to accept Africans as shipmates, but this does not pardon them from the shame of slavery. To pirates, African slaves were one more form of booty. From Seadog John Hawkins's first slave-selling voyages in the late 1500s to the blockade-running blackbirders of the Civil War, piracy has always been associated with the stink and sadness of slavery.*

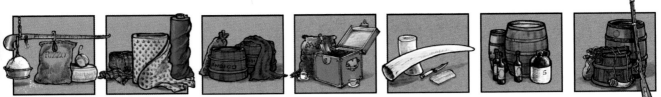

| FOOD | CLOTH | INDIGO | TEA & COFFEE | IVORY | RUM & WINE | GUNS & GUNPOWDER |

JEAN LAFITTE *was a charming, intelligent pirate (he would insist he was a privateer) who commanded a large navy and ruled the vast, swampy territory he called Barrattaria at the mouth of the Mississippi River (see page 8). He hated Spaniards and plundered their ships, but he would not raid ships of the young United States. While he was providing luxuries to the rich of New Orleans, tax free, from his pirate vessels, he was a dashing figure in New Orleans society, often dining with the governor—who was "officially" chasing him.*

Who were the Seadogs?

King Henry VIII of England recognized that his small island needed a large navy. This became even more important when, in 1531, he refused the authority of the Roman Catholic church and became a Protestant. Henry died before his new navy was strong. His oldest daughter, Mary, tried to solve the problem of defending England by marrying the king of Spain and returning England to Catholicism. (They called her Bloody Mary because she hanged and burned many Protestants.) She died only a few years later.

Henry's second daughter was crowned: Queen Elizabeth I. Like her father, she was a Protestant, and she shared his certainty that England needed a powerful navy. But England needed time to build it.

So Elizabeth commissioned privateers, "gentleman adventurers" who could afford to outfit a ship and pay a crew. She called them her Seadogs. She could not directly order them to harass Spain—no war had been declared. But she let them know what should be done. The Seadogs—pirates and rogues, every one—bought Elizabeth the time to build the Royal Navy and keep England independent.

SIR FRANCIS DRAKE *was called Elizabeth's Dragon. (Drake actually means "dragon.") He went to sea at twelve and was the finest of the Seadog mariners. He was the first English sailor to circumnavigate (sail all around) the globe. He borrowed 1,000 crowns, a small fortune, from Elizabeth and set out with a small fleet in 1577. On the way he pirated, raiding Spanish towns everywhere, seizing Spanish ships, and capturing important charts of unknown waters. He sailed to the west for South America and returned from the east, up the coast of Africa, bringing his queen an additional 46,000 crowns. Furious, Spain planned to send a great fleet of ships, the Spanish Armada, to conquer England. While the Spanish were preparing the invasion, Drake "singed the king of Spain's beard" by sailing into the Spanish port of Cádiz. He burned and sank two dozen ships and burned an especially important warehouse full of barrel staves. When Spain finally sailed in 1588, they had no good barrels; their food was bad and their water was tainted. Most of the invasion sailors were sick. In the week-long battle with the Spanish Armada, Drake—ever the pirate—paused to capture the Spanish flagship* Rosario *with its money chest.*

QUEEN ELIZABETH
KNIGHTS SEADOG
FRANCIS DRAKE

SIR WALTER RALEIGH *was a great favorite of Queen Elizabeth. He borrowed money from the queen to build his ship, the Ark Royal, and led the English fleet in its battle against the great Spanish Armada in 1588. Raleigh spent a lot of time in jail. Elizabeth threw him into the Tower of London for marrying one of her ladies-in-waiting, Bessie Throckmorton, without permission. She released him when one of his ships returned with a huge Spanish prize. After the queen's death, he was again thrown into prison on suspicion of plotting against the new king, James I. In prison he wrote his five-volume* History of the World. *Raleigh was released to fight against Spain one more time, then beheaded. His wife kept his head until she died, twenty-nine years later.*

SIR JOHN HAWKINS *was born into an English shipping family and went to sea as a boy. He understood ships and became a shipbuilder. Hawkins built a new kind of warship. It was light, fast, easy to handle, and carried many guns. These were the tough little men o' war that defeated the mammoth Spanish galleons. Hawkins was smart and inventive, but his reputation carries a dark stain: He started the slave trade. He bought captured tribesmen from chiefs on the African coast and sold them to the Spanish colonies in the New World.*

Who were the buccaneers?

THE SACK OF PANAMA

Pirates followed the gold. Around 1600, the richest prizes sailed from the treasure ports of the New World. Galleons heavy with gold, silver, and jewels set out from the Spanish Main, the mainland of Central and South America. They were bound for the open Atlantic and Spain, but first they had to pass through narrow passages between the islands of the Caribbean—perfect for pirate ambushes!

Deserters and shipwrecked sailors from many countries lived on the Caribbean shores. Many lived by hunting in the hills and preserving the meat in native smokehouses called "boucans." These shabby sailors rowed out to passing ships to sell their smoked meat, so they were called "boucaniers." The name buccaneer came to mean the bands of rough men in those parts.

In 1603, King James I of England canceled all English letters of marque. Privateering in the Caribbean was dead, but rich prizes still sailed for Spain. Ex-privateers formed a pirate navy of their own, based on the island of Hispaniola (present-day Haiti and the Dominican Republic). They called themselves the Brotherhood of the Coast, and they fought off Spanish attempts to root them out. The brotherhood welcomed Spanish deserters, convicts, outlaws, and escaped slaves. Some escaped African slaves even became pirate captains.

The buccaneers gave pirates a reputation for cruelty. The Spanish themselves were cruel, but the buccaneers served out even crueler treatment. Did they roast Spanish captives and make other Spaniards eat them? Probably not—many of the pirate legends that started with the buccaneers are exaggerated. Still, they were violent, lawless men greedy for gold and eager to make Spain suffer.

Sir Henry Morgan

GOLD, JADE AND JEWELS, much of it looted from the old Aztec, Maya, and Inca empires, made Spanish treasure chests fat.

GALLEONS were the Spanish treasure ships. They were large, stable, and fancy. They were good gun platforms in a broadside-to-broadside sea battle, but they were slow and awkward. Galleons were easy pickings for a surprise attack from a quick pirate schooner packed with vicious fighters.

HENRY MORGAN was the most famous of the buccaneer captains. He was violent and heartless, but so successful in attacking Spanish ships and treasure ports in Central America (and so wealthy because of it) that he was knighted and made governor of Jamaica. His greatest prize was sacking the Spanish treasure town of Portobelo in Panama. As governor, he pursued his old pirate friends and hanged them. Four years after he died, a great earthquake struck Jamaica, and his grave was swallowed up by the sea.

Did the freebooters wear shoe

Pirates in the colonial days of North America were not like t buccaneers. They had influential friends ashore, and they provided an important service. These pirates were called freebooters (from the Dutch vrijbuiter, "free booty"). They were mostly smugglers, supplying untaxed goods to grateful settlers on the coast of America. Freebooter vessels were welcome visitors most ports, especially the English colonies in North America. Some were even financed by investment groups of businessmen who outfitted the ships and bought letters of marque from dishonest officials.

Freebooters flourished because England tried to make its colonies profitable. Colonists grew weary o high taxes on imports. The American colonies were allowed to sell their own products to other nations, and prices were unfairly rigged. These infuriating taxes and restrictions led to the American Revolutio in 1776. Before then, freebooters—often respectable citizens—smuggled in goods under the noses of tax collectors.

The freebooters probably exaggerated the legend of their piratical cruelty. Ships would surrender quickly if they thought pirates might skin them aliv It's likely that many tales of their sea battles were coverups. They might pay a captain and crew to lool the other way while "pirates" unloaded their cargo holds.

Their most determined enemies were colonial officials who wanted their share of the taxes. Smart pirates bribed colonial governors from the booty.

BLACKBEARD

BLACKBEARD *was known in his home port of Bath, North Carolina, as the respectable mariner Captain Edward Teach (he had several other names). A large and powerful man, he cultivated a frightening look at sea, never cutting hair but braiding it in fantastic ringlets and pigtails. He commanded a small flee of pirate vessels. When he attacked a ship, he threaded burning slow-fuse through beard and hair to look even scarier.*

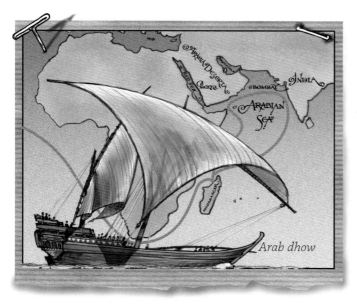

Arab dhow

THE PIRATE ROUND *was a profitable round trip between the American coast and the pirate lairs of Madagascar. The freebooters cruised the Red Sea and the Arabian Sea, snapping up Arab and Indian merchant vessels. It was not considered illegal or even immoral to plunder Muslim and Hindu ships. Some of the prizes were rich indeed. Pirate captain Henry Every captured the Gang I'Sawai in the Red Sea as it returned from a pilgrimage to Mecca. The booty was close to two million gold and silver pieces, plus jewels and the ransom for important Arab and Indian prisoners.*

CAPTAIN WILLIAM KIDD *was a mild family man who owned merchant ships, property, and a pew at Trinity Episcopal Church in New York City. A group of English earls and dukes persuaded him to capture pirates in the Arabian Sea aboard the* Adventure Galley. *Most of Kidd's American crew was pressed (forced into service) by the Royal Navy, leaving him criminals and lubbers. Kidd was hopeless: He insulted Royal Navy officials and attacked the wrong ships. His crew hated him. In frustration, Kidd whacked William Moore, his gunner, with a heavy bucket, killing him. He took the rich* Quedah Merchant, *an Armenian ship, and sold some of the cargo to pay off his crew. But the* Quedah Merchant's *captain was English! From another "prize," he got only a sack of peppercorns and a sack of coffee beans. When Kidd's crew deserted him for a more successful pirate ship, he left for America with his share of the* Quedah Merchant's *loot. He buried his treasure on Long Island before seeking a pardon in Boston. He was arrested and thrown in jail. Officials dug up his treasure. After three years alone in a London prison, lawyers finally consulted him two hours before his trial. None of the earls or dukes spoke up for him. He was sentenced to be hanged, for piracy and for killing his mutinous gunner.*

Capt William KIDD

HANGING KIDD *was as messy and ridiculous as his pirate cruise. He emerged from prison drunk. The first rope broke. The second held. His body was tarred and hung in chains for years beside the Thames River as an example of piracy and stupidity.*

I n the early 1800s, after the American Revolution and the Napoleonic Wars, it was obvious that nations needed secure sea lanes to trade with one another. It was also obvious that taxes should be paid for imports. The large nations of the world and their navies ran down the pirates and hanged them. There were still sea outlaws here and there—piracy goes on in remote parts of the world today. But modern piracy is the business of large corporations, not little crews of discontented sailors who promise to abide by their own sea rules.

Even when piracy flourished, it was a risky profession. Life aboard a ship was unhealthy. Germs had not been discovered yet, and often half a vessel's crew might die of typhoid, just because they didn't wash their hands. (Let this be a lesson to you.) In the tropics, thousands died of malaria and yellow fever. Some pirates died by drowning (very few could swim) or in common shipboard accidents. A large number died from sexually transmitted diseases. Pirates who died in battles were rare, but not as rare as old pirates.

> The schooners and their crews
> Have all been quiet laid to rest,
> A little south the sunset
> In the Islands of the Blest.

John Maesfield, "Tales of a Former Jolly Roger"

Where did all those pirates go

THE GIBBET *was worse than death for most pirates. After a condemned pirate had been hanged, his body was tarred to preserve it, then placed in its own specially made gibbet, a chain-and-iron cage that held the bones together and prevented friends from taking the body for burial. It would hang for years as a harsh example of piracy's reward.*

BURIED TREASURE? *Very few pirates made a huge amount of money, and they seldom buried their treasure. They spent most of the money. The few pirates who did take a fabulously rich prize put the money in banks or invested in snug little taverns near the sea. It's nice to think of gold and jewels waiting to be discovered on a treasure island far away, and there may be a few chests of doubloons and pieces of eight (Spanish gold coins) just under a rock in your backyard. Most pirates felt, however, that they might very well be killed in a battle or, worse, caught and hanged. "A short life, and a happy one" was their motto, and they spent what they stole very quickly.*

BLACKBEARD'S HEAD *Governor Alexander Spotswood of Virginia hated Blackbeard. He requested a special expedition against the infamous pirate. In 1718 two sloops-of-war tracked down Blackbeard's vessel, Queen Anne's Revenge, in a shallow inlet. Royal Navy Lieutenant Robert Maynard attacked. After a long duel, and after being shot more than six times, the pirate was killed. His head was cut off and hung at the yardarm of Maynard's sloop on the return voyage. Governor Spotswood could, at last, sleep easily.*

WINE PORTER COMMONS

OLD PIRATES *were rare. Disease, hanging, shipwreck, and battles killed off most pirates early. They were too old to sail, all their loot had been spent, their shipmates were dead. Old pirates would have been a pitiful lot. But what stories they must have told!*

Index

Copyright © 2004 by Jan Adkins
Published by Roaring Brook Press
Roaring Brook Press is a division of Holtzbrinck Publishing Holdings
Limited Partnership
2 Old New Milford Road, Brookfield, Connecticut 06804
All rights reserved

Distributed in Canada by H. B. Fenn and Company Ltd.

Cataloging-in-Publication Data is on file at the Library of Congress
ISBN: 1-59643-007-9

Roaring Brook Press books are available for special promotions
and premiums.
For details contact: Director of Special Markets, Holtzbrinck Publishers.

First Edition September 2004
Book design by John Grandits
Printed in the United States of America
10 9 8 7 6 5 4 3 2 1

Pirate words

aloft *above the deck, in the rigging*

avast *"stop," shortened from "hold fast"*

belay that *"stop," "put an end to that"; a line was belayed (fastened down) when a line was tight enough*

Black Ship *the Portuguese treasure ship that sailed once a year between Macao and Acapulco, also called the Manila Galleon*

black spot *warning from a pirate crew that the recipient must amend his ways or die*

blackbirder *a slave boat*

buccaneer *a Caribbean pirate in the 16th and 17th centuries*

cut of his jib *first impression, from sailors' ability to recognize types of ship from a great distance by the way their sails were fashioned*

cutlass *a short, slightly curved sword*

dead man's chest *when a sailor died, the possessions in his sea chest were auctioned off to his shipmates and the empty chest was a reminder of the lost companion*

doubloon *a gold Spanish coin*

flying angels *chain shot: two round shot connected by a short length of chain that "flew"—whirled through the air—to cut up a ship's rigging*

freebooter *a pirate of the Caribbean or the East African Coast in the 17th to 18th centuries*

grape shot *several plum-sized balls used as spreading cannon shot against rigging or crew*

grog *rum with water, a drink served out daily to Royal Navy sailors until the 19th century*

hardtack *dried (hard) biscuit, stored in watertight barrels or tins; also "soft tack," conventional soft bread baked ashore (ovens took too much fuel to use at sea)*

head *the sailor's toilet or "seat of ease" in the bows (head) of the ship*

hornpipe *an intricate, athletic sailor's jig, danced without partner. Its name comes from an ancient instrument resembling the modern oboe.*

keelhaul *a terrible and usually fatal punishment once common in the Royal Navy: an offending sailor was bound by lines and dragged under the ship, rubbing against sharp barnacles and copper seams; sometimes performed thwartships (side to side) or, worse, fore and aft (lengthwise, almost surely fatal)*

Lascar *sailor from the Middle East*

leeward *(pronounced LOO-ward) in the direction toward which the wind is blowing*

loose cannon *a person or situation of great danger; a heavy cannon sliding loose on the deck of a ship posed a terrible danger of crashing through the ship's hull to sink the vessel*

lubber *ancient term for a clumsy person; clumsy sailor; also landlubber, a great insult*

man o' war *an official warship; also man o' war fashion, run strictly and neatly*

Mecca *also Mekka and Mekkah, the holy city of Islam to which every Muslim is bound to attempt a pilgrimage at least once in his or her life*

pieces of eight *Spanish coins worth eight reale (each reale was worth about thirty grams of silver)*

prize *a ship or other property captured in battle*

rum *a strong alcoholic drink usually made in the Caribbean from fermented, distilled molasses*

scurvy *a potentially deadly shipboard sickness caused by lack of vitamins in fresh vegetables and fruit; also, from this disease, anything sickly or disgusting*

salamagundi *a spicy dish of several meats, vegetables, eggs, &c, favored by pirates*

slops *sailor's clothes*

Spanish Main *originally the Central and South American Coast ruled by Spain, this term came to mean the Caribbean Ocean sailed by Spanish galleons*

steady as she goes *continue to steer in the same direction*

swab *a lowly or unskillful person, since swabbing (mopping) the deck was a job for the least skillful sailors*

three sheets to the wind *inebriated, drunk; from the practice of signaling distress by loosening one sheet (line that controls a sail) to allow a sail to flap, in mild distress, two sheets for severe distress; anyone who is "three sheets to the wind" is wobbling and navigating with difficulty*

weigh anchor *to leave, from pulling up (weighing) the anchor that holds a ship in port*

whiff of grape *a devastating load of grape shot fired at a vessel*

windward *in the direction from which the wind is blowing*